Love Never Wrongs

Written and illustrated by Steven Noel Sikes

Text copyright © 2025 by Steven Noel Sikes
All rights reserved.

Unconquered Publishing

ISBN 979-8-9989476-2-9

No part of this book may be reproduced, or stored in a retrieval system, or transmitted in any form or by any means, electronic, mechanical, photocopying, recording, or otherwise, without express written permission of the author.

Cover design by Steven Noel Sikes
Cover illustration by Steven Noel Sikes

LOVE NEVER WRONGS

Written and Illustrated by
STEVEN NOEL SIKES

for Natalie

the best part of me

Contents

IGNUS ORITUR

She Stands at the Edge
Paper Choices
The Musical Heart
A Loss for Words
Third Floor Branham
The Artist
The Broken Stoic
Bah Bah Bah

IMPERIUM FLAMMAE

The Price
The Probability Problem
The Documentarian
The Power of Water
Metamorphosis
World Knots
10,000 Hours

CINIS AMORIS

This is the Page
I Am There
The Closed Door
Values
The Spoken Things
The Boy Who Cried Love

IGNUS ORITUR

She Stands At The Edge

In all my life I have had but one recurring dream, the dream of a woman standing at the edge of a rocky outcropping. She is looking out over the valley below, and the rising sun's golden hues are intermittently ethereal behind swift motion of the low billowing clouds. Their shadows swiftly undulating over the mountains surrounding us like my hands over her feminine form. She is shrouded in a robe or blanket that flows down from her beautiful shoulders and is carried into the air as the gusts catch her. She is strong and fearsome to behold, and her majestic dark lochs flow freely also. The scent of fresh mountain air tinged with the slightest metallic note indicates that a heavy storm is fast approaching. I feel she is the very storm herself, and I the lightning to her thunder. Our hearts feel connected through some hidden force that defies time and distance. I know we belong together, that we are destiny incarnate, but I cannot see her face. Why can't I ever see her face?

And then I wake once more to the emptiness of a world without her. So I escape to the mountains whenever possible, and always hope to catch a glimpse of her, to feel the power of that lofty place from time immemorial. And again I am recharged - for a while.

Paper Choices

Standing there in the paper isle of the local craft store, I feel such indecision. Which type of paper should I choose? Which will add just the right touch of gravitas and elegant flare to the message I must write for her?

Should I choose a noir theme?
Gold embossed stationary?
Or should it be aged parchment with a waxen seal?

I choose the latter for what I am feeling must show its timeless quality, the purity of the lettering through the ages represented within the fibers of the page.

No matter what, the message is written on it will be monumentally inadequate to the task of conveying the depths of my feelings for her.

The Musical Heart

She walks and sways as her music plays,
Her inner feelings overflowing.
Her bright eyes blast forth luminous rays.
My love for her seems ever-growing.

Had I enough time to spend
Listening to her majestic sound
I would listen through my final end
And continue 'neath the ground.

The shape she takes as she plucks the strings
Defines beauty for all to see,
And as those hypnotic chords ring
I know she sings for me.

The truest thing that my heart now knows
Is how I shall always adore her.

A Loss For Words

An opened mouth that shuts again and smiles,
A deep breath and a rapid glance away,
That upward tilt of your jawline
As you contemplate a phrase you won't say.

A look back at me, first smiling,
Then deadly serious
When you see me staring in wonderment
You see the sadness of my battered heart.

You open your mouth again to speak,
But nothing exits;
Your eyes scream at decibels off the scale
Everything that you want from me.

You look down again and back up slightly
Out at me from under those curls
And the depths of the universe cannot compare
To the enveloping vastness of your soul.

Third Floor Branham

Walking through mall today I passed a tea shop and the scent that wafted through the air to my nose was as a teleportation machine. Mid walk I was transported through time and space to the little single dorm room on the third floor of Branham Hall some 20 years prior. She was fortunate, most everyone else in the entire college had to room with at least one other student, or commute like me, but the RA for that floor was rooming with their friend instead of getting the coveted space.

My eyes were creeping open, trying to adjust to the horizontal light peeping through the mildly damaged metallic blinds that were as old as the building itself, meaning they were installed in the late Triassic. My mind takes a few beats to figure out the unusual surroundings. There is a stack of bowls in the sink across the room, and more than a few cheap mugs stacked nearby, a few with overly ornate chopsticks poking out from their rims. The walls have posters with great works of art, and some were from music groups of a decidedly dower variety. The keys to an ancient Volvo are strewn on the futon next to a stack of unfolded laundry. "Cuzco, Who names a car after a cartoon llama" I thought?

The smell of lavender and other difficult to place aromas mix in my first breaths of the morning, the lavender coming from the mugs, the shampoo, and basically anything else you can get scented that was present in the tiny universe where I now found myself. I roll my head to my right and see her long flowing black hair draped over her face, a face smooshed against my bicep where her cute crinkled nose and pouting lips peer out through the strands. Her breathing is slow and peaceful, and her side sleeping body raises her right shoulder in a rhythmic fashion, the sleeping bag blanket she is under is clutched tighter than the grab handle in Cuzco when I ride shotgun.

She then puts her arm and leg over me, leaning in, gentle and warm. Her large, dark brown, Cuban eyes open beneath her hair and in that moment I want children for the first time in my life.

The Artist

He has an easel for a heart,
And watercolor runs through his veins,
He'll paint you into his picture
On the canvas in his mind.
His gallery is getting crowded
With all the paintings that he's made
Of the people who've wandered his halls,
But left the show before the end.
There's one piece that's near the very back,
It sits amongst the lonely,
With his finest touch he's drawn
"The Moon and Stars who Stole My Heart,"
There are half-finished works of art,
Sketches of every person he's met.
Some people are only a notebook doodle
While others are veritable masterpieces,
Thousands of tiny brush strokes
They've left across his heart.

You might wonder why he's done this,
Why draw the people he's once known?
But he hopes one day he'll mean enough
For someone to draw him too.

THE BROKEN STOIC

THOUGHTS CONTROLLED GAVE
MASTERY OVER SUFFERING.

UNDERSTANDING OF MY LACK OF CONTROL
ALLOWED THE REMOVAL OF
THE NEGATIVE STING.

REDUCTION OF NEEDS
SET ME FREE FROM WANT

YET I SUFFER, HURT, AND AM ENSLAVED
TO THE KNOWLEDGE
THAT YOU ARE OUT THERE.

IT IS MY
MOST PLEASANT PAIN.

Bah bah bah

Tucked entirely in one arm
You spoke yours tiny words of charm.
"Bah bah bah," you said to me.
"Um hmm bah bah," I said to thee.

With a bright-eyed countenance
You cut those eyes in sideways glance.
"Bah bah Bah bah," you said to me.
"Oh no, bah bah," I said to thee.

Then sternly staring with intent
You knew exactly what I meant
"Bah bah baaaah," you said to me.
"Da da bah bah," I said to thee.

Now you stand and reach my shoulder,
And even though we both are older
You never needed words to know
How your father loves you so.

IMPERIUM FLAMMAE

The Price

Coffee - $2.50

Journal and pen - $25.99

Divorce - $23,500, three years, and primary custody of my children.

Child ransom payments - $1000 per month over twelve years. Complete physical, emotional, and financial devastation.

Rebuilding from nothing - Strained family relationships, a career change, therapy, countless hours at the gym, coffee, a journal and a pen.

Knowledge of self with peace of heart and mind - Priceless.

The Probability Problem

Most people do not really understand probability. Many think that any given thing either will or will not happen. They think the odds are always 50/50. They think they should play the lottery when the jackpot is at its peak amount, that traveling by car is safer than flying. They could not be more inaccurate.

When I sip my coffee, looking out at the visiting hoards of tourists to my once sleepy little town, I see the countless people and know the probabilities.

4 out of 100 will be arrested.
1 in 5 will die of cancer.
1 in 3 will die of cardiovascular disease.
1 in 100 will possess an equivalent IQ or higher.

This means that the likelihood that any given person I meet would be both as intelligent and also the opposite sex is essentially 1 in 200. Further still the probability that they are available is much lower, and the chance that they would be physically attractive even lower, and attracted to me lower still.

It is a unique problem, to know it is ridiculously unlikely that I will meet someone I can share the kind of connection I desire. To know that acknowledgment of these facts is considered condescending rather than honest.

I have flipped the coin hoping it will land on its edge.

The Documentarian

Suited up in Tyvec, boots taped at the seam to prevent contamination from the toxic sludge, respirator squeezing lines on her face, piercing blue eyes flaring behind her goggles, she surveys the damage.

All day she labors to dig, carry, scrape away the aftermath; anything she can do to help. Today she is not an interviewer or producer. Today she says little and simply works. One of the first in and last out, today she is one of the best examples of humanity I have ever witnessed. So I take her photo to document that she was there.

The Power of Water

Last year I spent the day sitting on a rock in the middle of a river flowing through small mountain town. Last year it brought me peace in a troubled time. I drew in my book, and the trickling sound of water drowned out the noise of my mind and gave me the solitude I needed to move forward.

Today the entire town is gone, wiped from the map due to that same river. The buildings are washed away, the road through the town almost missing entirely. A town that had been there for nearly a century was there one day and gone the next.

The things that give us comfort can be powerful; indeed so powerful that we may take their tranquility for granted and allow their power to destroy us.

Metamorphosis

It came on slowly, a hint of a feeling here and there, an uneasy tingling in my soul; then it popped into the forefront of my consciousness, that I had grown so far beyond you that you couldn't or wouldn't catch up. The things with which you concerned yourself were so trivial and meaningless that I could not even pretend to care. The endless chattering over people, or the shock at events; none of these compared to the sparring over ideas that my mind craved.

The epiphany was obvious, glaring at me in my mind's eye. Our pathways would forever need to part for self preservation. I was not then angry, nor was I even upset; I was a the sort of melancholic that comes with the peace of having new direction, of knowing I would need to continue alone. The chrysalis seal was broken. I could not change back.

World Knots

Everywhere has a set of coordinates to mark out its location in the three dimensions of space. When you think of meeting someone though, this is not enough information, you need a temporal coordinate also. Without knowing when in the history of time to meet, you could both arrive and never see each other. The term used for the sum of your spatial and temporal coordinates is called your World Line. Everywhere you go and when you are there is a point in the line. When you return to places you like the line can corkscrew but never loop exactly back due to the different time. Time dilation near massive objects at ridiculous speeds still can only let you see where you have already been. You cannot change the past.

I like to think that when we encounter people that our world lines make a fabric of sorts. The areas where we spend the most time being knotted together. Sometimes those may be very haggard and frayed, where we were when we suffered pain or loss or setback; where we fought battles with other lines and with our own. Other times the threads are loose and rarely touch when we are not accepted or lonely; times when we are grasping for purchase to keep from unravelling. Most important of all are when we find the people we love. When those world lines meet they form a woven cloth of the finest silken joy. They appear as a world plane to the hearts of those outside of the intertwined. Knotted together with great skill and care, they create something stronger than the individual components could have ever been on their own.

10,000 hours

There is a theory that 10,000 hours of deliberate practice can gain almost anyone, regardless of initial capability, mastery of a given skill.

If you want to master the violin? It will take 10,000+ hours to achieve what most would consider mastery.

If you desire to be a great chess player, you have to practice with a deliberate intensity for 10,000 hours.

If the perfect golf swing is a skill you desperately want, you are in luck if you have 10,000 hours to devote to the task.

When I tell you I have drawn in notebooks for that long and longer, I trust it shows.

So trust when I say I have spent orders of magnitude more time missing you.

CINIS AMORIS

This is the page

This is the page where my poem should have been.

These are the letters that might have lived within,

But here I am thinking back on just how far we went,

I cannot bear that the words won't come

And can't convey what it meant.

This is the stanza where I professed my ever undying love.

This is the line that rhymed with "the myriad stars above."

This is the empty space where I would have written more

About how much you mean to me, and how when we fly we soar.

But now my mind is shocked and numb,

The figures do not equal the sum.

I cannot fill this page with words that won't come

Because my heart breaks so.

I can only try to tell you that I already miss a future

The two of us will never know.

I am there

I am there
With her in my dreams,
The setting sun's glare
Shedding golden beams
Across her face,
The face of perfection,
Overlooking this beautiful place
Motioning me in her direction.
Wind in the rustling grass,
New stars on distant horizon,
It is then we focus
Her eyes and mine on
Each other's outstretched arms of love
To hold one another.
I cannot reach, she is above.
Away she flies
She can stay no longer
For morning grows nigh,
Still my thoughts dwell in her.
I see her now though I am awake.
These euphoric visions
I cannot shake.
I will soldier on,
I will find her in
The place that she has gone,
In heaven I will be with her again.
And then my one, my love, my life shall see
That I am there.

The Closed Door

I pray you never know the singular sorrow

That wells up in your chest

Forcing you to close

Your child's bedroom door

Because walking by the open, empty room,

Where once there had been laughter, joy,

Closet monsters, and bedtime stories;

And now exists silence and the

Exquisite agony that can only come from

The corruption of a beloved memory,

Is more than you have the strength to

Allow yourself to entertain when the

Child is forcibly absent.

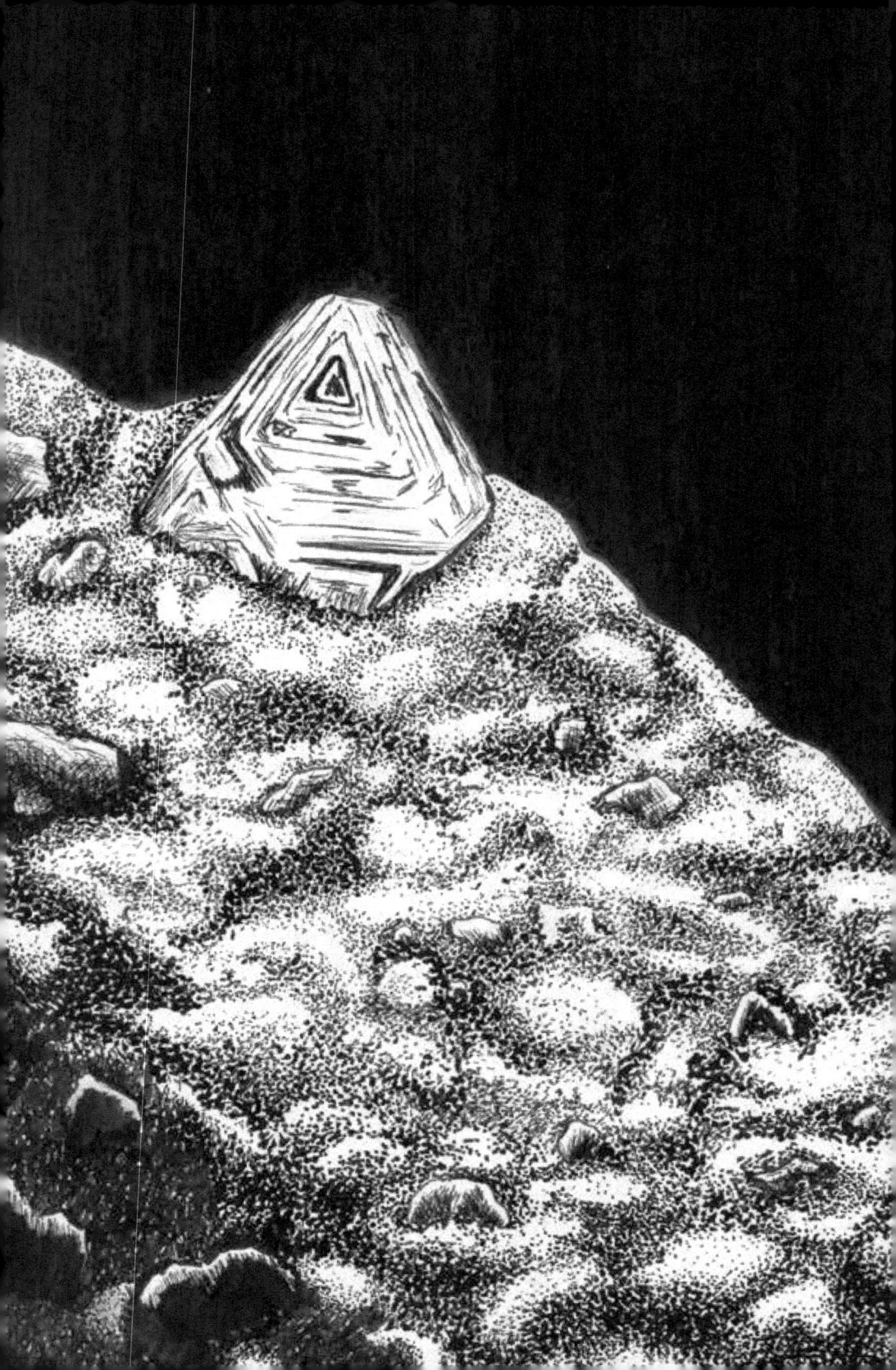

Values

From youngest days I did learn
How to let my passions burn,
Adding to my brainy core
All the facts and figures for
Adding to my value.

I exercised my physical measure
And found in competition pleasure;
The warmth of a victorious heat,
Or the subterranean depths of defeat
Added to my value.

The practices of chivalrous knights,
The best ways to win my fights,
The viewing of the Dutch masters,
Kipling's triumphs and disasters
All added to my value.

Now a diamond cut from the rough
From feeling I was not enough.
Yet I miss that most desired touch.
You fear that I will cost too much.
Now you walk right past my value.

The Spoken Things

Once you told me you broke down in a town on the way across country with your sister.

You looked so happy talking about the way that everything just worked out and how you met some wonderfully fun locals.

You told me another time about how you would make trips to your family's property near a lake back home, how you loved the area so dearly.

You told me how you cherished new experiences and the majesty of the natural world.

You told me during the total solar eclipse that you loved me.

I wondered about all the things you never told me, the things you held back.

Now I wonder how I believed even the words you did speak.

The Boy Who Cried Love

There once was a boy who attended University and frequented his local coffee shop. He would draw and write and think great thoughts, and every now and then a young lady would approach him while he was scribbling in his notebook. "What are you doing?" She would ask. "I am pouring out my soul." He would reply. Moved by the beauty of this the young lady would sit and talk further. Eventually the boy and the girl would arrange another get together. Over time the boy would pour forth his soul towards that girl alone. When he was overcome with the flood he would tell her he loved her. Often the young lady would say the same in return.

Friends and family far and wide would congratulate them on their wonderful news, but each time the couple would part as the flood of love broke through the dams placed in its path by the girl's understanding of the word. Some would say that he never loved her, that he just wanted something else. Over time this process would repeat, and each time the friends and family would congratulate less and less as they had done before, and each girl would doubt even more that his love overflowed for her. They had seen it before. And so it was that when the boy met the greatest love of his life, and the love he had for her would wash over the mountain tops, she could not believe him.

You see, she, like their friends and family, only understood love to be finite; that he had a limited supply and would have to further dilute each time he used the word love. She thought he couldn't love her with all his heart if he had given pieces of it away to others from his past.

But love does not work like that. Love is infinity. Love can by multiplied and not divided. What she did not know is that he loved them all, and that in no way made his love for her any less. It was the greatest love he had ever experienced, and the irony was that it was not received because he had cried love too often before.

Love, when not received, undergoes a type of metamorphosis. It changes into resentment, tension, anxiety, and pain. Receive it when it flows to you. Let love wash over you like the tide. The beach does not concern itself with whom it shared the ocean.

www.ingramcontent.com/pod-product-compliance
Lightning Source LLC
Chambersburg PA
CBHW070038070426
42449CB00012BA/3090